My Uncle, Captain Starlight

By Pamela Rushby
Illustrated by Nigel Buchanan

Pearson Australia
(a division of Pearson Australia Group Pty Ltd)
707 Collins Street, Melbourne, Victoria 3008
PO Box 23360, Melbourne, Victoria 8012
www.pearson.com.au

First published 2014 by Pearson Australia
2018 2017 2016
10 9 8 7 6 5 4 3 2

Publisher: Dian Faulisi
Project Managers: Tamara Pirois and Rachel Davis
Editor: Beth Zeme
Cover and series designer: Jenny Grigg
Designers: Jennifer Johnston and Nina Heryanto
Copyright & Pictures Editor: Katy Murenu
Mac Operator: Rob Curulli
Cover art: Nigel Buchanan
Illustrator: Nigel Buchanan
Printed in Australia by the SOS Print - Media Group

ISBN 978 1 4860 1465 1

Pearson Australia Group Pty Ltd ABN 40 004 245 943

Disclaimer
Some of the images used in *My Uncle, Captain Starlight* might have associations with deceased Indigenous Australians. Please be aware that these images might cause sadness or distress in Aboriginal or Torres Strait Islander communities.

Contents

Chapter 1

Going to Wombunderry

Kids have all kinds of uncles. Sporty uncles who play cricket with you. Generous uncles who give you sixpence or a shilling. Funny uncles who tell jokes. Uncles with bushy beards that tickle when they kiss you. Uncles who live near, and uncles who live far away. Uncles who drive trains, and uncles who shear sheep. Uncles who work in shops, and uncles who work in banks. But my uncle was special. Really special. He was … a bushranger.

My Mam and I went to live with my Uncle Harry in the year 1870, when I was 10 years old, after father died. At least, my Mam said he must have died. He went away to look for work shearing, and he never came back. We only had one letter. That was not long after he'd left. And then there was nothing.

Soon, we had no money. My Mam tried to find work, but it was hard. At last she wrote to our only relative, her brother – my Uncle Harry.

Uncle Harry replied at once, and his letter said, 'Annie, you and Tom get onto a Cobb & Co. coach at once and come to live with me.' There was money with the letter for our tickets. Mam was so relieved she cried and cried. I was glad Mam wouldn't have to worry any more, and excited for an adventure in the country.

Uncle Harry lived far, far out in western Queensland, past Windorah and Jundah. He had a small run called Wombunderry on Cooper Creek, where he raised cattle. It took us days on the Cobb & Co. coach to reach Wombunderry. The horses pulled us further and further west, into country that grew drier and more desolate with every mile.

Black cockatoos with bright red under their tails sat on fences and screamed at us. Kangaroos bolted away from the road. Dust flew up and hung, thick and red, behind the coach. I loved it! Mam wasn't quite so enthusiastic, but she was so happy to have a home to go to so she didn't much mind.

Uncle Harry met us at Jundah and drove us the rest of the way in a cart. "How are things for you?" Mam asked Uncle Harry. "Are you doing well?"

Uncle Harry sighed. “Times are hard,” he said. “Especially for people like me, with small runs. There’s been no rain, and stock prices are low. I haven’t got many cattle left. I’ve had to take on work as a carrier, driving goods from Tambo to a big property called Bowen Downs.”

Mam looked worried. “Oh dear,” she said. “Are you sure you can afford to have us live with you?”

"It's all right," Uncle Harry said. "We'll be fine. Good times are bound to come again. They always do."

I looked around. "But there are lots of cattle here, Uncle Harry," I said. "Are they yours?"

"I wish they were, Tom," said Uncle Harry. "No, they all belong to Bowen Downs. It's owned by a huge pastoral company."

We passed a small building at a crossroads. There were children playing outside, and they all stopped and stared at us.

"That's the school," said Uncle Harry. "You'll be going there, Tom."

"The school!" I said. Somehow, I hadn't thought there'd be a school way out here. "Oh. Do I have to go to school?"

"Yes, you do," said Mam and Uncle Harry together.

A young woman came out of the school and rang a bell, and the children lined up to go inside. They kept staring at us, though, and so did the young woman. "Hello, Mr Redford," she called.

Uncle Harry raised his hat. "Hello, Miss O'Hara," he replied. He turned to Mam and me. "Miss O'Hara's the school teacher," he said.

Mam looked at the pretty young school teacher, and then at Uncle Harry. "Hmmm," she said.

Uncle Harry laughed. “Now don’t you go putting two and two together and getting five, Annie,” he said. “Miss O’Hara’s just a friend.”

I’d been thinking fast. “Wouldn’t it be better if I helped you on Wombunderry, Uncle Harry?” I said. “I don’t really need to go to school. I’ve been for four years already! I can read and write.”

"You need more than that, Tom," said Uncle Harry. "Otherwise, you'll end up like me: sitting on a bit of barren dirt, praying for rain, and working as a carrier. Go to school and you'll do better than that." He laughed. "You could aim at owning a station as big as Bowen Downs, and running thousands of cattle. Then you'd be doing all right!"

Chapter 2

Cattle duffing and poddy dodging

So that was that. I had to go to school. It wasn't too bad, though. The other kids were friendly and Miss O'Hara was nice. She didn't yell at us, she very rarely used the cane and she read us lots of poems and stories. She was very keen on reading and writing. She wanted us to write something ourselves every day. That was why we each had a notebook that Miss O'Hara called a 'journal'.

Miss O'Hara said she didn't mind what we wrote. It could be about anything!

"Write about anything that you find interesting," Miss O'Hara said.

I found lots of things about life at Wombunderry interesting and never had trouble finding something to write about. I wrote about the animals and plants around us, and I also wrote about the work Uncle Harry did around the property and his cattle.

As the drought went on, I started to write about the creek drying up and the tank getting very low on water. I noticed that Uncle Harry's cattle were getting thin and bony, but the cattle on Bowen Downs were still fat and healthy. This was because Bowen Downs had lots more water. I put that in my journal too.

One evening Uncle Harry had visitors: Mr McKenzie, Mr McPherson, Mr Doudney and Mr Brooke. They all worked as carriers, like Uncle Harry, taking goods from Tambo to Bowen Downs. They brought a few brown bottles with them, and as the evening went on they started to talk. First, they grumbled about the drought and how their cattle were all going to die if rain didn't come soon. Then, they started to talk about the number of fat, healthy cattle on Bowen Downs.

"Think what a price they'd fetch in Adelaide!" said Mr McKenzie.

"They'd never miss a few," said Mr McPherson.

Uncle Harry looked thoughtful.

"That's right," said Mr Doudney. "Bowen Downs doesn't have enough stockmen to keep track of all the cattle."

There was a silence. Then, "We could do it, you know," said Uncle Harry. "We could round up some Bowen Downs cattle and drive them overland to Adelaide and sell them."

The men all looked at each other. "That's cattle stealing," said Mr Brooke.

"Not really, it's cattle duffing," said Uncle Harry , shrugging his shoulders. "There's a difference. It's just the same as poddy dodging. Everyone does that."

I was sitting at the table, writing in my journal, but I was listening to them too. "What's poddy dodging?" I asked.

They all jumped. "Forgot you were there, Tom," said Uncle Harry.

"Poddy dodging? Well, it's catching unbranded calves and putting your brand on them."

"You mean catching *other people's* unbranded calves?" I asked. "And branding them as your own? Isn't that stealing?"

The men all looked uncomfortable. "No, it's not really stealing," said Mr McKenzie. "It's just – well, relocating some cattle."

"Everyone does it," said Mr McPherson. "If you're too careless to round up your calves and brand them, you deserve to lose them."

"Oh," I said. "I see. That's interesting."

The men kept talking.

"Drive cattle to Adelaide? From here?" Mr Doudney said. "That's impossible."

"He's right," said Mr Brooke. "That's more than 1200 miles of the toughest, most isolated country in Australia. It can't be done."

Uncle Harry disagreed. "It could, you know," he said. "The season's been good, down that way. There'd be plenty of feed and water along the route. The Barcoo, Cooper Creek, Strzelecki Creek – that'd be the way to go. It could be done."

The men all looked at each other again.

By the end of the evening, they'd decided that, for a start, they'd round up some Bowen Downs cattle and keep them in small, hidden yards. If the cattle weren't missed, then they'd decide whether they'd attempt the big drive to Adelaide.

It was all very interesting. I wrote it all down in my journal.

Chapter 3

A distinctive white bull

Uncle Harry and his friends built some cattle yards, hidden in the bush. They began to take cattle from Bowen Downs and put them into the yards. They waited to see if the stockmen on Bowen Downs noticed that cattle were missing, but no one said anything. So they took some more.

I went to the hidden yards with Uncle Harry one day and found that a very big white bull had come in with a mob Mr Doudney had taken.

"That's not a good thing," said Uncle Harry. "That bull's too distinctive. You need to let it go."

"I tried," said Mr Doudney. "It won't go – it wants to stay with the mob. I can't chase it away."

"Oh, well," said Uncle Harry. "We'll get rid of it later."

They collected more and more cattle, until they had a mob of around a thousand head. It was time to make up their minds whether they'd attempt the drive – or not.

The next day, I came up against a problem. Miss O'Hara asked to see our journals. Usually she didn't check them. She just wanted us to write. But now, she wanted to make sure we were actually writing.

I'd been writing a lot. That was the problem. I'd written all about Uncle Harry and his friends, and their plans. And by now I'd figured out that what they were planning wasn't really legal. I couldn't show Miss O'Hara what I'd written!

I tried to tear some of the pages out, and then write some other different, harmless entries, but I didn't have enough time. My journal looked as if some days I'd written nothing, other days just a line or two.

Miss O'Hara was very disappointed with my journal. "I know you've been writing lots more than this, Tom," she said. "Where is it?"

Very reluctantly, I showed Miss O'Hara the pages I'd torn out. "I have been writing more," I said. "But, well, you see…"

Miss O'Hara glanced at the pages. She read some of them more closely.

"Oh!" she said. "Oh. I see the problem, Tom." She handed the pages back. "I don't think I need to read any more," she said.

I took the pages from her with a great sigh of relief.

"Tom," Miss O'Hara said. I turned back. "I think you should keep your journal very, very secret from now on."

"Oh, I will, Miss O'Hara. I will!" And we smiled at each other.

Uncle Harry and his friends had a meeting one evening. Mr McPherson and Mr McKenzie kept saying it was impossible. They said no one had ever driven cattle from Jundah to Adelaide before and they'd never make it. Uncle Harry, Mr Doudney and Mr Brooke kept replying that of course they could make it, and someone had to be the first to do it. I fell asleep before they'd finished talking.

They must have made a decision, though, because I woke up the next morning and Uncle Harry was gone.

Mam and I knew where he'd gone, of course, and I think Miss O'Hara guessed, but if anyone asked we said that Uncle Harry had gone away to find work. In other words, we kept our mouths shut.

Then, a week later, I saw Mr McPherson and Mr McKenzie in Jundah. "What are you doing here?" I asked. "I thought you'd gone with Uncle Harry to … um, to find work."

"We did," said Mr McPherson. "But we came back. It's a crazy scheme, they'll never make it. We left before we got to the Barcoo."

"It's only ten years since Burke and Wills died in that godforsaken country," said Mr McKenzie. "We'll probably never hear from them again."

I certainly hoped we would.

Chapter 4

Arrested!

Soon enough, we did hear from them. A few weeks later, Mam and I got a note from Uncle Harry. It was very carefully worded, in case it fell into the wrong hands, but it said he was at a station near Artracoona, in South Australia. So they'd made it that far! That was amazing!

"We parted from our old friend Mr White here," the note said. I knew what that meant. They'd sold the white bull! That was good, because that bull was just too easy to recognise.

Then we heard nothing more, until months later, when we received a postcard. It was from Adelaide! It said:

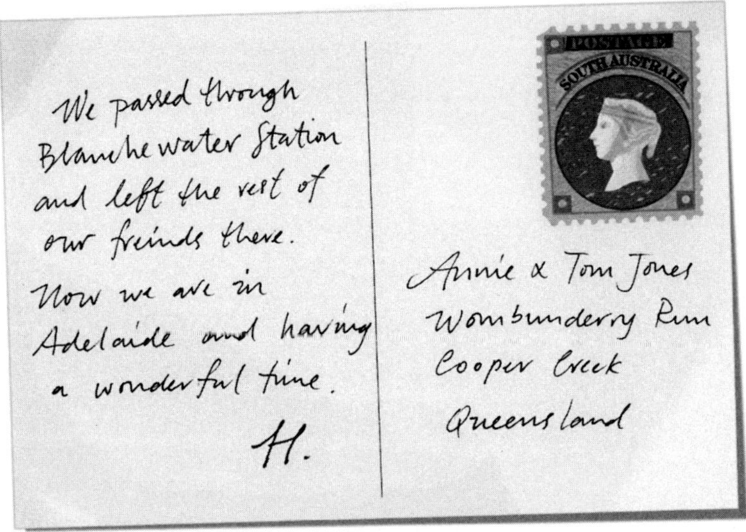

We passed through Blanchewater Station and left the rest of our freinds there. Now we are in Adelaide and having a wonderful time.

H.

Annie & Tom Jones
Wombunderry Run
Cooper Creek
Queensland

So Uncle Harry, Mr Doudney and Mr Brooke were safe in Adelaide. They'd succeeded in driving the cattle all the way there, through the harsh, unexplored bush. They must have sold the cattle at Blanchewater Station, I thought.

Mam and I were delighted – and relieved – that they'd have plenty of money from the sale. They'd be having a fine time in Adelaide.

Back home, Mr McKenzie and Mr McPherson were not having such a good time.

Mr McKenzie had kept on duffing cattle from Bowen Downs – and this time, the missing cattle had been noticed. The cattle had been tracked to Mr McKenzie's run, and he'd been arrested.

The owners of Bowen Downs ordered a count of their cattle and discovered how many were missing, the white bull among them.

The police were called in, and Mr McPherson and Mr McKenzie were interviewed. They told the police everything. Everything!

I was disgusted with them. "Traitors! They think they'll get off lightly if they tell," I said to Miss O'Hara.

Miss O'Hara sighed. "They may be right," she said.

Now that the police knew what had happened, they got onto the trail. With the help of Aboriginal trackers, they managed to follow the tracks Uncle Harry and his friends had left all the way to South Australia, where they found the white bull.

The bull was sent back to Tambo, as evidence, and Mr McKenzie and Mr McPherson were found guilty of cattle stealing. Serves them right, I thought.

Now I was really worried about Uncle Harry. I didn't want him put in jail. But it looked as if Uncle Harry was too clever for the police. Well, he was for a while. The police couldn't find him for a long time, but a year later, Uncle Harry was found and arrested.

Mam and I heard that Uncle Harry was going to be charged in the District Court at Roma in February. We looked at each other. Roma was a long way away. "But we have to be there for Uncle Harry!" I said. Mam agreed we must.

Everyone was talking about the case. Some people, like big property owners, said that Uncle Harry was a cattle thief and should be thrown in jail.

Others pointed out that what Uncle Harry and his friends had done was a great droving feat. They'd driven a thousand head of cattle well over a thousand miles through some of the roughest country in Australia. They'd had no maps; they'd had to rely on their instincts and bushmanship. And along the way they'd only lost about 25 head of cattle – some of which they'd killed for food.

If it wasn't for that distinctive white bull, they might never have been caught at all. A lot of people admired my Uncle Harry's skill and daring – and I was one of them.

When February came, Mam and I travelled to Roma to support Uncle Harry at the trial. The whole town was talking about it, which made us extremely nervous.

We were allowed to see Uncle Harry, just for a short while. Mam hugged him. I hugged him. "Look at you, Tom – how you've grown!" Uncle Harry said. "You'll be able to come droving with me soon!" That was a joke, I think, but I truly hoped I could, some day. That's if Uncle Harry didn't get thrown in jail for years and years.

And it was certainly looking as though Harry might go to prison. Mr McKenzie was the chief witness against him. In fact, there were lots of witnesses against him, and there wasn't a single witness for him. Things looked bad for Uncle Harry, very bad.

Chapter 5

Not guilty, Your Honour

Mam and I sat in the hot, crowded courtroom for the trial. Mam looked more and more worried as the day went on. There wasn't a single person to say a good word for Uncle Harry. Mam and I kept looking at the jury, twelve men from the town, to see what they were thinking. We couldn't tell.

The judge knew how he felt, though. When the lawyers had finished talking, the judge said the evidence showed that Uncle Harry was guilty, and that that was the verdict the jury should bring back.

He sent them off to discuss it. The jury was only away for an hour. "This can't be good," Mam whispered. "They made up their minds so quickly."

The foreman of the jury stood up to tell the court their verdict. Mam and I gripped each other's hands. We waited for the jury to say, 'Guilty', and for Uncle Harry to be sent away to jail. I was convinced this was what was going to happen to Uncle Harry.

So, when the foreman said, “Not guilty, Your Honour,” I couldn’t believe I’d heard right.

The crowd in the courtroom erupted in cheers, shouts and whistles. They were all cheering for Uncle Harry! The judge’s face turned red. He leant forward in his chair and scowled at the jury. “I thank God that the verdict is yours, gentlemen, and not mine,” he growled, standing up and stamping out of the courtroom.

The people in the court – except the prosecution lawyers – just laughed at the judge and cheered Uncle Harry even louder.

Mam and I pushed our way through the crowd towards Uncle Harry. In the crush, I was separated from Mam, and I stopped and leant against a wall to get out of the surging crowd.

There was a door beside me. It was ajar. I could hear the judge inside, talking to someone angrily, and I stood listening for a moment.

"I can't believe they found that absolute criminal innocent! It's obviously a case of one lot of cattle thieves trying another!" the judge spluttered.

"It's an outrage! This certainly would not have happened in England!" I heard another voice reply.

I smiled, very happy that we were in Australia.

The crowd cleared a little, and I found my way to Uncle Harry. Men were slapping him on the back, shaking his hand and congratulating him. "Why?" I asked him. "Why did they let you go?"

The foreman of the jury was shaking Uncle Harry's hand, and he grinned at me. "Young fellow, your uncle's one of the best bushmen in the country!" he said.

"He did an impossible thing!" piped in another juror. "We couldn't lock him up for it. Not just because he relocated a few head of cattle!"

"The judge isn't happy," I said.

All the men laughed. "Dare say he isn't," one said. "These big pastoral companies! They never think what it's like for the ordinary people. The little people."

"So, Uncle Harry's a hero?" I said.

The men laughed again. "That he is!" they said.

Uncle Harry had had enough. "Come on," he said to Mam and me. "Let's go home."

Chapter 6

Captain Starlight

So my Uncle Harry was released. But he didn't stop relocating cattle – and horses, too. Over the years, he was taken to court several times for horse theft (not that he saw it as theft). And eventually he was sent to jail in Brisbane for 18 months. That seemed to settle him down, because after that he led a law-abiding life.

He died in 1901, trying to cross a flooded creek.

By then, my Uncle Harry had become famous all over Australia.

In 1888, a man called Rolf Boldrewood wrote a book about bushrangers. It was called *Robbery Under Arms*, and it was about a bushranger called Captain Starlight.

I read the book, and I couldn't believe it. Mr Boldrewood might have called the main character Captain Starlight, but some of the amazing things Captain Starlight did were exactly what my uncle had done.

"Captain Starlight!" I said to myself. "This book isn't about any Captain Starlight! It's about Harry Redford, my Uncle Harry."

My Uncle Harry had been a cattle duffer and a poddy dodger, it's true. But he was also an outstanding bushman and cattle drover. He was a legend.

And I was very, very proud of him.